MAINLY TRAINS

Denis Dunstone

INTRODUCTION

This book contains a series of articles written for the magazine of the National Transport Trust between 1995 and 2012. They are, as the title suggests, mainly about trains, but what they have in common is that most touch on one or more of the differing aspects of preservation. The reasons for preserving anything are numerous and there are many opinions within the world of transport. Some argue for 'importance' trying to define 'importance' as an objective quality, but it inevitably tends to be subjective and to vary over time. Some have personal, sentimental or at best nostalgic reasons. Sometimes there are lessons to be learned and taught to future generations. But it is mostly because items are liked for one reason or another, by enough people that the effort to preserve is stimulated. Preferably it is restoration to working order, for transport needs to move and it is said that it is easier to preserve an airplane if it flies, than if it sits quietly decomposing in a museum.

The book concludes with the background to the ultimate preservation of the Brighton Belle electric train, initiated by the National Transport Trust.

ROYAL JUBILEES

The celebration of royal jubilees within the transport sector has been dominated by the railways. In 1935 there was one aviation example, the Monospar ST-25, named the Jubilee and numbered 25 in honour of the reign of King George V.

In 1887, the year of Queen Victoria's Golden Jubilee, a fleet of four wheeled carriages was built for the Metropolitan Railway. One has survived because it was sold to a minor railway in the West Country and is currently being restored by the London Transport Museum. It is known as the Jubilee Carriage.

In 1897 the Great Western Railway built for Queen Victoria a magnificent new Royal Train in celebration of her Diamond Jubilee.

On the same occasion, after the festivities in London, Queen Victoria travelled north in the LNWR Royal Train, bound for Balmoral. The railways concerned, the LNWR and Caledonian, joined in the celebrations with a unique tribute. The LNWR abandoned their usual blackberry-black livery for the royal train locomotive. Instead No. 2053 'Greater Britain' was painted red to work the London to Crewe leg of the journey. At Crewe it was replaced by No. 2054 'Queen Empress' painted white. At Carlisle the LNWR handed over to the Caledonian whose locomotives were appropriately blue already.

'Queen Empress' about to be relieved by the Caledonian locomotive at Carlisle. This was named 'Victoria' for the occasion.

I commissioned this painting by Mike Turner.

'Queen Empress' Photo GH Platt collection.

In 1934 a new class of locomotives was introduced by the LMS. The following year the class was selected to celebrate the Silver Jubilee of King George V. The latest member of the class was turned out in gloss black with chromium plated bright-work and named 'Silver Jubilee', seen below on a cigarette card.

JAYWICK MINIATURE RAILWAY

There have been and still are countless miniature railways in gardens all over the country. By contrast with narrow gauge railways, they are normally built for private use, for fun or for pleasure, but rarely as a commercial carrier. The better known public examples such as the Romney, the Ravenglass and the Fairburn operate mainly as tourist lines. Perhaps unique therefore was this one mile long line whose purpose was to function as a public carrier in Clacton on the Essex cost, offering a year-round timetable service. It may also hold the record for being the shortest-lived public railway.

It was opened in 1936 at the initiative of a developer who was building houses for commuters and retired people on the outskirts of Clacton. Public transport was sparse so an 18" gauge railway was built. It ran from a station on the sea wall for nearly a mile , then descended at 1 : 100 through a 60 ft. long tunnel under a pre-historic barrow to a terminus at a place known as Crossways.

Today the construction of such a line would entail countless applications, inspections, approvals, hearings, and appeals, all at great expense. And as for burrowing under an ancient burial ground - forget it !

The staff of three operated a half-hourly service starting at 8.30.a.m and at an average speed of 35 m.p.h. provided a seating capacity for 2,000 passengers a day in two 18 ft. long coaches. After closure these went to the Ravenglass. Fares were collected on the platform, 6d return for adults, 4d. for children. The railway lasted until 1940 when wartime conditions forced its closure.

The first locomotive was a miniature version of Stirling's Great Northern single driver, but it suffered from the hard water and was replaced in 1938 by a Sentinel two cylinder locomotive with a 'Lune Valley' type boiler. This had its own water treatment plant and could raise steam in eight minutes from cold.

The Stirling Single was unused for many years, being bought by the workshop superintendent at Cambridge University.

2010

LOST OPPORTUNITIES

We are so accustomed to seeing wonderful examples of all kinds of transport beautifully restored that it is salutary now and then to be reminded that many good things have been lost, and that only continuing vigilance will prevent further losses. The attached photograph taken in 1953 by Alan Jarvis shows what happened to a Red & White bus before it finally disappeared.. This was a particularly unfortunate case as there are few if any surviving examples of a rare centre door Duple body on an Albion chassis as seen in the second picture. Red & White, was once the largest independent bus company in Britain.

[Albion

BUS STATIONS

Often overlooked yet at one time central to many people's lives, bus stations present a sad story in preservation. Normally sited in town centres where land values are high, they have presented attractive sites for development. Although often of some architectural interest, this was normally insufficient to engender public support or listing. Some notable examples have been lost for this or other reasons, as for example in Derby and Bournemouth. Purpose-built survivors are rare. The most well-known of these is Victoria Coach Station, while in the provinces there is a good example at Taunton. At Abergavenny in south Wales a rare purpose-built bus station remains intact but in alternative use.

Another remarkable survivor is at Preston. This massive structure was built in 1969 and is a striking building made from pre-cast concrete units. A multi-storey car park is above the ground level bus station. It is threatened with destruction as its annual maintenance is £300,000 and its refurbishment is estimated at £23m. English Heritage has twice recommended listing, but the local authority was adamant that it must go in spite of pressure from the SPAB, the 20th Century Society and the RIBA..

It was eventually saved not on technical or architectural grounds but by the pressure of well orchestrated public opinion.

Victoria Coach Station

Abergavenny Bus Station ca. 1950 by Gwyn Briwnant Jones.

A NORTHERN LINE EXTENSION IN HEREFORDSHIRE ?

Railway preservation takes many forms so it should not be too much of a surprise to find a Northern Line carriage on the Welsh Border. After all the railway on the Isle of Wight has been using tube stock for many years and a sailor on arrival at Alderney will see a tube carriage hauled by a diesel locomotive. The tube car in Broadoak Herefordshire is on a stretch of track in a back garden where the destination indicator is changed every day.

It has been said that railway preservation is communal and compelled to be where there is a railway. In this case the nearest railway is 20 miles away.

1998

YOUR TRAM IS READY, SIR.

Sweden has a well developed collection of preserved transport, treated by the authorities as part of the order of life. Thus, when the tram system was closed down in Stockholm, a tramway preservation society was offered the operation of a key tourist tram route- for nothing. The only condition was that if they ceased to operate it, the concession would cease.

Perhaps in a highly taxed country people expect government to take actions left to individuals in less taxed countries like Britain. For instance the Swedish Minister of Defence is a volunteer guard on a preserved railway. As the Chairman of the Tramway Preservation Society concluded his welcome speech to the international preservation organisation Fedecrail, he was handed a key, 'Your tram is ready, sir'. He slipped away to drive the 10.14.

1997

A GEORGE V IN ESSEX

In a range of locomotives employed on the 10 and a quarter inch gauge Audley End Miniature Railway is a replica of 'Loyalty', a member of the former LNWR George V class. Although it is a miniature built in 1992, what strikes the observer is the gorgeous LMS livery and the simple well proportioned lines of what was at one time one of the most popular classes of locomotive in the country.

One of the perverse aspects of preservation is how accidental has been the choice of locomotives to be preserved. It seems unjust that among all those preserved Bulleid Southern Railway Pacifics there is not one LNWR passenger locomotive.

At least we have a miniature version which belongs to Lord Braybrooke, an admirer of the LNWR and its locomotives.

THE VALUE OF PRESERVATION

A case has arisen in France where the failure to preserve is possibly going to lead to recreating a closed railway for environmental reasons. Though it will be more of a re-creation than a restoration.

On 1 May 1907 a steam railway was opened to a station at 1415 m. near the top of Puy de Dome in the Massif Central. The line, some 15 km long led from the centre of Clermont Ferrand, partially along existing roads. Steam propulsion was chosen, partly to avoid unsightly electric plant, but also at the request of the meteorologists operating an observatory at the summit. Adhesion and additional braking was provided by what was called the 'systeme Hanscotte' which consisted of two wheels set horizontally beneath the locomotive pressing against a central third rail. It must have been a spectacular ride as to reach the summit the line circled the mountain over more than 360 degrees.

Due to the poor economics part of the line was electrified near the bottom in 1911, but World War I prevented further work. 1911 was the only year when a surplus was generated. Although the line was closed during the war and the locomotives and rails were seized by the army for use at the front, it was reopened in 1923, only to close again in 1925.

Now the private car has presented a problem. With over 450,000 visitors a year to the summit, half by car, the car is now banned access in July and August. In 2003 consideration was given to rebuilding the railway.
A five km. rack railway was opened in 2012

TO DARJEELING BY TRAIN

In 1999 UNESCO cited the Darjeeling Himalaya Railway as a World Heritage Site, putting it on a par with the Pyramids, the Taj Mahal, Greenwich, and Blaenavon in South Wales. This places the burden on the host country, in this case India, to preserve the railway infrastructure for ever.

In 2000 a party from Britain visited India to celebrate this event. The party assembled in Delhi and visited the Rail Museum there. This had been established due to the efforts of an Englishman, Mike Satow, while serving as the representative of ICI in India. He later became Chairman of the TT. The high point of the visit was a tour in a railway carriage hauled by the oldest working steam engine in the world, 'Fairy Queen', built in 1855 in England.

After a lunch party in the garden of the Minister of State for Railways, the visitors moved by chartered air-conditioned train to Calcutta. The reception there was tumultuous, the renown of the party being enhanced by the presence of Sir Adrian Cadbury. Folk dancing and music preceded supper in the former residence of the Maharajah of Birdwan. On the following day there was a cruise on the Hoogli River. The party were touched by the warmth of the welcome in Calacutta and left feeling it was a much more handsome, vibrant and thriving place than its reputation allowed.

Another over-night train took the party to New Jalpaiguri where the DHR begins. In a distance of 58 miles the 2 ft. gauge line climbs some 7000 ft. The journey was exciting with wonderful views and was enlivened by two de-railments and an engine failure due to a shortage of water. In places the climb is so steep that the builders had to resort to zig-zags and loops. Darjeeling was developed at the end of the 19th century as the summer retreat for the civil service when the Indian capital was still Calcutta. It is still a charming hill station.

The preservation of the DHR is an example of cooperation between state and private sectors, and foreigners. It started in 1994 with the creation of a foundation by a local businessman, owner of the Windamere Hotel in Darjeeling. They were supported by the local authorities and Indian Railways and the English 'Friends of the DHR'. The DHR Society has 500 members. Much diplomatic negotiation was needed to preserve the railway, and the efforts of Benedict Cadbury, son of Sir Adrian, were acclaimed during the visit. The Indian Railways were to invest £1m. in track repairs and efforts were to be made to increase tourism.

THE SARGAN EIGHT

This railway which links Serbia and Bosnia was so-called as the track describes a figure-of-eight at one point. The 760 m. gauge railway was completed in 1925 after overcoming a change in height from 400 m. to 800 m. in a distance of 35 km. There are 20 tunnels, the longest being 1.66 km. The railway was closed in 1974 and the track was ripped up. While Yugoslavia existed as a state it concentrated its tourism on the coast and paid scant attention to the

Two levels of track on the pass

development of inland tourism. It has now been realised that a narrow gauge railway traversing a mountain range with impressive ascents and descents through tunnels could attract tourists. Through the energy of a finance director of Serbian Railways, 13 km. of the highest part of the route has been restored and the station at Mokra Gora near the Bosnian frontier has become an attractive tourist centre. One of the Austrian-built 0-8-2 locomotives has been restored and steam trains operate again.

0-8-2 locomotive at Mokra Gora

LIFE WITHOUT PRESERVATION

In Malta, between 1883 and 1931 a meter gauge steam railway operated over some five miles between Valletta and the second city, Medina. It had over time 10 British built steam engines and ran some 10 trains a day in each direction on a journey taking about half an hour. It was never very profitable and eventually the government took it over, whereupon it made losses until it was closed. The locomotives and carriages were sold at auction and went to an Italian scrap yard in 1931. At that time railway preservation had hardly begun, even in England. The North Eastern Railway had a collection at York and there were museums in Norway, Germany and Japan. Preservation by private individuals was rare and so nothing of Malta's railway was preserved. In 1955 when the writer was a guest of the RN in Malta, there was no sign of it.

In a forward to a book published in 1988 entitled 'The Malta Railway' the writers bewail the absence of more deliberately preserved relics than the occasional building, a tunnel, rails used as fencing, and some street names.

Manning Wardle locomotive at Valletta.

Many regretted that personal relics collected by their ancestors who worked on the railway had been lost or just thrown away. Records and evidence disappeared, and it was left to the authors to attempt to piece together from disparate sources some some idea of what the railway was like and what it contributed to island life.

Today we are aware of the merits of preservation and the commercial possibilities. Yet we are in danger of being overwhelmed by the mass of material of all kinds with which we are surrounded, and sometimes fail to hold on to items which could later have become prized.

LONDON TRANSPORT AT WAR

Michael Baker wrote 'London Transport in the Blitz' in 2010. It is informative and has some unfamiliar photographs, many from the LT Museum. The author's personal recollections bring the book alive. He lived in Croydon which suffered seriously from bombing and he recalls a range of personal experiences such as an ST bus overtaking a convoy of tanks and Bren carriers on the Brighton Road, a meeting with the engineer charged with designing the towed gas containers, the radio programmes, air raid sirens on the day war was declared, the experiences of evacuees, the dimming of vehicle lights by masking, the protective material stuck to bus windows, and so forth. He also records that deaths on the road rose 40% due to the blackout with a total of 11,000 a year compared with 3,000 in 2008.

Fuel restrictions of 25% led to a reduction in the bus fleet; Green Line coaches were converted into ambulances. Among deeds of heroism one noble driver moved buses out of a blazing garage. Illuminating is the chapter on life in the tube shelters where 150,000 people were fed.

The book concludes with a list of wartime vehicles surviving in preservation. Included was LT1076, a rare single decker so-called 'scooter'.

LT 1076 was bought at auction in 1995 by the LT Museum for £1250. Half of that sum was provided by the TT.

RAILWAY ANNIVERSARIES

Forty years on from 1968 there is hardly a railway journal in the land which has overlooked the end of main line steam in Britain. To be specific they mean main line standard gauge scheduled steam locomotive-hauled passenger train on British Rail. This was, it is generally agreed the 20.50 from Preston to Blackpool on the 4th August 1968, hauled by 'Black Five' No. 45212, which was subsequently preserved. A week later three other 'Black fives' hauled what were called the '15 Guinea Specials' which were run to mark the end of steam haulage.

'Last' scheduled steam train 4 August 1968.

This is tricky territory. Arguably steam haulage never ceased. The Vale of Rheidol, owned by BR, continues to this day to run steam engines on its narrow gauge railway, as do the Snowdon Mountain and the Romney. Even during the ban on steam, Flying Scotsman was able to continue to run on the main line due to a contractual right.

The problem of definition arises frequently over the start of railways. If by 'rail' is included any means of bearing weight and reducing friction then wooden rails of the 17th century may be considered. Many would maintain that the Surrey Iron Railway was the world's first public railway. However as was revealed in the correspondence stirred by this article when it first appeared, although its Act of Parliament of 1801 was the first, it was not the first to open. This honour fell to the Carmarthenshire Railway or Tramroad whose Act was passed in 1802. It was operational by May 1803, two months ahead of the Surrey Iron.

In 1804 Trevithick ran the first steam railway engine on the Penydarren Tramroad. In 1807 the world's first passenger railway was the Oystermouth Railway which was powered by horses. In 1812 the Middleton Colliery Railway was the first to operate commercially with mechanical propulsion. Back in 1758 it had been the first railway authorised by an Act of Parliament. It was also the first standard gauge heritage railway, running a train in June 1960 just before the Bluebell started running timetabled passenger trains. In 1825 the Stockton & Darlington was the first steam hauled public railway, while in 1830 the Liverpool & Manchester was the first steam hauled double track public passenger railway. In the same year the Canterbury & Whitstable was the first regular passenger steam railway. In 1832 the Festiniog was the first to be incorporated by Act of Parliament and in 1836 the London & Greenwich was the first in London and the first in the world to serve a capital city.

The demise of steam on public railways occurred at a remarkably similar time around the world. Dutch Railways were the first switching from steam in 1958, USA and Canada 1960, Belgium 1966, France 1967, Switzerland 1968, Norway and Denmark 1970. Sweden 1972, Spain 1975, and Austria 1976.

Further afield they lasted longer : South Africa 1990, Thailand 1992, India 2000, China 2005. Poland retains one line though more as a preservation exercise than a genuine steam line.

BY No.3 BUS TO BUCKINGHAM PALACE

I had been to the TT office in Lambeth Road and was making my way back to the West End. I was accustomed to using route 3 to Trafalgar Square as it passed the TT office on its way from Crystal Palace to Oxford Circus. On the day in question there were demonstrations in Parliament Square, so the No.3 was diverted from Lambeth Bridge through Westminster, up Grosvenor Place and then along Piccadilly to join its usual route at the bottom of Regent Street. However, at Hyde Park corner the driver, who looked a complete stranger to London, missed the turning to Piccadilly and went on round to Grosvenor Place, then back along the west side of Buckingham Palace.

At this stage I realised that he might be lost. Fortunately I was sitting on the lower deck, so I went up to him and asked him if he knew the way. He reluctantly admitted that he did not, and by this time we were moving fast along the back of Buckingham Palace and in the wrong lane for making a right turn back to Victoria. So we turned left along Buckingham Palace Road.

This is not on any bus route as commercial vehicles are banned from the area at the front of Buckingham Palace, including the Mall and Constitution Hill. It was now plain that we were about to venture into forbidden territory. Near the end of Buckingham Palace Road the driver called out with a note of desperation in his voice, "Where now Boss?"

Where indeed ? Birdcage Walk would have led to Parliament Square but that was closed to traffic. It would have to be the Mall or Constitution Hill. There was no way of avoiding the prohibited area, so I told him to bear left across the front of the Palace.

The quickest way back to his route would have been along the Mall and through Admiralty Arch into Trafalgar Square. However I then had a worrying thought. Would this bus fit beneath the arch ? I had forgotten that in the 1946 Victory Parade a fleet of London Transport double-deckers had driven down the Mall and under the Arch, and so, being uncertain and unwilling to be responsible for removing the top deck of a bus, I decided to play it safe. Accordingly I told the driver to turn left up Constitution Hill. At the top there was some evident surprise on the faces of bus and taxi drivers that a bus should appear from that direction, but we managed to find the Piccadilly exit and on the way to Piccadilly Circus I asked the driver if he could now manage on his own. As far as I know he did, as I left him there.

2011

PAPAL TRAIN FOR HIRE

The Papal train was hired by Caritas, the Catholic charity, to take a party of guests on a special trip from the Vatican to Orvieto in Umbria. It was the first time the train had been used without the Pope on board. It was hauled by a preserved 2-6-2 locomotive built in Italy in 1915, and the carriages were a formation which had been dedicated for use by the Popes.

Papal train in the Vatican Station

In 1934 a Lateran Treaty between the Holy See and the Italian State provided for the construction of a railway into the Vatican. It is the shortest national line in the world. Mussolini arranged for a station to be built in the Vatican gardens and it was formally opened in 1934. In the walls of the Vatican massive iron doors were fitted which slide back to allow trains through the wall. The first Pope to use the railway was Pope John xxiii.

2011

TRANSPORT TREASURES IN TRIESTE

In the far north east of Italy and in territory which was until 1918 part of the Austro-Hungarian Empire, Trieste lies on a large bay surrounded by hills. At one time the principal port of the Austrian Empire, it was served by two railways from Austria, each with its own terminal station near the waterfront. They crossed at a village called Villa Opicina high above the city. When Italy acquired this territory in 1918 it included land to the east called Istria. In 1945 this became part of Yugoslavia. Trieste became an outpost of Italy bordered by then Communist Yugoslavia and its eastward railway connections became unusable.

As a result the more recent station nearest the harbour, Campo Marzio, which was connected to Istria, became redundant. It was leased to enthusiasts who made it into a railway museum. With maps, ephemera, models, railway relics, locomotives and carriages it relates the complex railway history of Trieste.

The Hungarian locomotive on the next page witnesses this history, Istria now in Croatia having been part of Hungary until 1918.

2010

Trieste is also notable for its last surviving tramway which runs from near the remaining station to Villa Opicina, 343 m. above. Built initially as a cog tramway in 1902 with overhead electricity supply, it was converted in 1928 to the funicular system at the steeper parts with special tractor vehicles to haul the trams. It survived World War II and continues today.

CRYSTAL PALACE LOW LEVEL, STATION

One of the most interesting stations in the London area is on the south side of the hill on which the Crystal Palace stood, after its removal from Hyde Park in 1851. In order to bring the large crowds which were expected to the site, eventually two railway stations served it. The first was Low Level which started as a Brighton line terminus in 1854. It stood at the end of a short spur off the main line to Brighton from London Bridge. The South Eastern built their terminus higher up the hill with no connection. It closed in 1954.

By 1970 it was expected that the residual traffic at Low Level would not justify its survival and an alternative use was under consideration. This coincided with the debate as to the future of the National Transport Museum at Clapham. It lay on a site owned by BR and ripe for development. Jennie Lee who was the Transport Minister at the time, was keen to move it to York where the former North Eastern Railway Museum was already established. The Transport Trust and others were keen to keep it in London as a museum of transport. A change of government gave the TT an opportunity to secure a change of heart. Lord Eccles, Paymaster General, responsible for the Arts, invited proposals for a

comprehensive scheme on a site in the London area, with rail connection, room for all the Clapham exhibits, and scope for expansion, all to be subject to the condition that the costs could be covered.
The TT in cooperation with the Clapham Society and Sir Robert McAlpine & Sons put forward a scheme estimated to cost £515,000. While £500,000 could be realised form the Clapham site, a further £6,000 would be available for housing the British Transport Records to be removed from Paddington. The value of the site at Crystal Palace was estimated at £25,000, so the project more than covered its costs. There would have been six tracks for rail exhibits and the road vehicles could have been accommodated on the first floor. There was a goods yard suitable for a turntable and for diesel and electric locomotives and one and a half miles of track suitable for steam train running. There was space enough for a tram shed and track, and access to the race track where vintage vehicles could run.
The scheme foundered because BR hesitated to close lines and LT were pressing for a solution. They accepted the TT suggestion of moving the Museum to Syon Park. Some of the railway material moved to York.

Crystal Palace Low Level would have eventually become too small for the museum.

LANCASTER CANAL

This canal linked Lancaster with Preston and Kendal. For a brief interval between 1833 and 1846 it had a unique passenger service. However it became a victim of railway competition. When the Lancaster & Preston Railway opened in 1840, the canal company took up the challenge, reduced its fares by half and actually took over the running of the railway. Completion of the railway to Carlisle in 1846 spelt the end.

It had however put up a spirited defence. Because the canal was unusually straight, it was possible to tow vessels quite quickly. Four packet boats each over 72 ft. long and 7 ft. wide and carrying up to 70 passengers, were hauled by two galloping horses at an average speed of 9 m.p.h. and a maximum of 14 m.p.h. Food and drinks were served from a small galley. The horses, controlled by a postillion were changed every four miles, and the master steered in the stern. Other vessels were understandably required to give way.

The Lancaster Museum preserves the memory with some powerful images.

2007

View forward in one of the boats

A reconstructed packet boat in its setting

RAILWAY PRESERVATION IN AMERICA

Comparison of Charleston in south Carolina with Liverpool might be felt extreme, but this southern city with its smart 18th century houses and tidy streets, surviving with elegance from a turbulent past, does near comparison, for it was here that one of the earliest railways in America was born.

In a joint venture between the Natioanl Railway Historical Society and the city council, a museum has been built to house a replica of America's first home-built and successful steam engine, called 'The Best Friend of Charleston'. It was so called because the railway enable Charleston to recover cotton trade earlier lost to Savannah.

The South Carolina Canal and Railroad was founded in 1827 and when completed in 1833 was the longest in the world at 136 miles. Construction began in 1830 following a visit by the engineer to George Stephenson. However before committing the company to steam propulsion the engineer tried other forms. He first experimented with sails and achieved a speed of 15 m.p.h. with a load of 13 people and 3 tons of iron. He claimed to have managed to sail up-wind to within four points of the wind, an achievement of which many a yachtsman would be proud.

He then placed a horse on a tread-mill and although this was reasonably effective he argued that, whereas there was little chance of improving the horse, a steam engine might reasonably be improved over time.

The decision in 1830 to employ a steam engine for both passenger and goods trains is claimed to be the first in the world. It was built that year in New York and operated successfully until the boiler burst. The driver had held down the safety valve while using the turn-table in order to save steam. The driver was injured but the locomotive was replaced.

Close to the museum a number of railway buildings have been preserved, but the railway itself is now a highway.

THE BERMUDA SLOOP

Although the term 'Bermuda rig' is familiar in the boating world as the name for a triangular sailed single masted sloop, its origins are less known.

The Bermuda sloop was developed in Bermuda soon after the islands were settled in the 17th century. The Governor at the time employed a Dutch boat builder, whose ship had been wrecked on the rocks of Bermuda. The Dutch had developed a design of boat with two sloping masts from a Moorish boat with lateen sails. The Bermuda sloop became the dominant sailing vessel for trading to and from Bermuda and then much further away. Being fast and able to sail upwind they were as useful for piracy as for trade. During the 18th century as many as 1,000 were built in Bermuda.

The RN developed the design, adding a mast, and it was one such, HMS Pickle, which bore the news of Trafalgar back to England in 1805.

Back in Bermuda the design was used for general cargo carrying and for fishing as motor vehicles were banned in Bermuda until after World War II. The last survivor, 'Shamrock', has just been restored. With a big sail, raked mast, long bowsprit, and shallow draft she is fast but tricky to sail.

2009

The casual posture belies the skill required

LINCOLNSHIRE VINTAGE VEHICLES

This organisation achieved its 50 years anniversary in 2010. Its history has instructive experience for transport preservation generally.

It was born of one man's enthusiasm assisted in a major way by the donation of a 1929 Leyland Lion single decker. It had been withdrawn in 1949 but had been retained as a snow plough. Like many transport relics it was saved by having an alternative use. In 1985 Lincoln City Council chose it as an object for youth training and, beautifully restored, it was used for city sight-seeing.

As early as 1962 the Society had the vision to see the need for covered accommodation. In 1970 an early Leyland TD1 double decker was restored, and all its vehicles, which now include some private cars, are kept in perfect condition and used for local tourism and national events. My favourite in the collection was a 1939 SS Jaguar. My recollection of these cars was that reliability was not their strong point. This one behaved perfectly when used on a test drive. It was in fact privately owned but kept by the society for a modest rental in accordance with the society's policy.

2010

Leyland TD1

1939 SS Jaguar

Leyland Lion

HAPPY ENDING

The Nord 4-6-0 No. 3.628, later 230 D116 was built in 1911 by Henschell & Co for express passenger work. In spite of working in the Amiens area during World War I, it survived, and remained in that area throughout World War II. It was one of the last of its class to remain in service, finally operating local services around Boulogne until 1964. The French Railway Museum rejected it, prefering another member of the class which had been built in France. Somehow D116 survived until 1972 when it was bought by a British group and taken to Ashford.

The Ashford project ran into problems in 1975, whereupon the locomotive, now restored to its original Nord livery, was moved to the Nene Valley Railway. This was done at dead of night as passage through the Dartford tunnel was slow with only inches to spare.

It hauled the first train on the NVR in 1977. It was then bought by the Science Museum for the National Collection and completely overhauled, and then leased back to the NVR for the next 10 years.

The complexity of its controls meant that there were only a few drivers passed to operate it, and this limited its use.

When the 10 years expired it stood idle at the NVR.

After a change of policy at the Science Museum, it was offered for sale. It was bought by the French preservation society AJECTA and returned to France in 2009.

rapatriée de Grande-Bretagne, la 230 D 116 lors de son acheminement par route depuis Cherbourg et à son arrivée au dépôt Ajecta de Longueville (mai 2009) ;

côtoyant des locomotives électriques, une 230 D dans les dernières années d'activité de la série.

échouent ainsi, en 2006, à récolter la somme nécessaire. D'autres projets verront le jour (tentatives de souscriptions, mise en vente sur eBay...), mais rien de bien concret.

Le retour de la « Frenchie »

C'est à ce moment que l'Ajecta décide, en toute discrétion, d'un éventuel rapatriement de la locomotive en France, et, grâce au don d'un généreux membre, s'en porte acquéreur. Les 9 et 10 mai 2008, elle reçoit des mains du propriétaire le manche du régulateur, la passation est organisée. Le transfert est toute-

…pension à …borough

sont, pour beaucoup d'entre eux, stockés au triage de Peterborough, certains étant préservés par des

DEEPEST NORTHUMBERLAND

In the heart of Northumberland there is a Heritage Centre based on the former station at Bellingham, 12 miles north of Hexham. This was the largest settlement on the one time Border Counties Railway. This independent concern started in 1855 as a means of connecting the mineral workings of the North Tyne valley with the Newcastle & Carlisle Railway at a junction west of Hexham. It later obtained authority to extend to the North British 'Waverley Route' at Riccarton Junction.

Before it was completed the NBR bought the Border Counties thus gaining the right to gain access to Newcastle over this 42 mile single track railway. Much survives since closure in 1958 except for 10 miles under Kielder Water.

The route can be followed with the help of tell-tale embankments, bridges, and cuttings, and that amazingly endurable railway post and wire fencing. Most of the stations are detectable if not intact and at Reedsmouth Junction it is still possible to work out the layout of track. This was the junction for Rothbury and Morpeth. A large engine shed still stands, serving as a cow shed. It was used during World War II as a shelter for some important preserved locomotives, including 'City of Truro'.
In the Heritage Centre at Bellingham there is a large collection of railwayana and an 0-gauge model of Reedsmouth Junction. There is also the contents of an early photographer's shop, with maps, photographs, and artefacts from the iron mining activity and local agriculture. There is a particularly rich stock of photographs held on computers. The whole is well presented and merits a large detour.

COURTESY

Overleaf is a letter of apology from Imperial Airways. It is notable not only for the detailed care applied in responding but also for the evidence that even in 1931 Persia or Iran was a difficult country to deal with.

IMPERIAL AIRWAYS LTD.

S: IMPAIRLIM, LONDON.
E: VICTORIA 2211.

AIRWAY TERMINUS,
VICTORIA STATION,
(CONTINENTAL DEPARTURES)
LONDON, S.W.1.

HB/PH/447

2nd September, 1931

Dear Sir,

Lingeh Forced Landing - August 28th.

I have to acknowledge with very many thanks the receipt of your letter of the 1st September. We very greatly appreciate the tone in which you write and would assure you that we are only too glad to receive criticism that is made in the helpful spirit in which your letter is written.

The photographs, too, are not only excellent in themselves, but give the clearest possible indication of the softness of the sand at Lingeh and bring home the local circumstances much better than a great deal of description would do.

With regard to Jask wireless, I regret to say that it has been the cause of continuous complaint from us to the Persian Government ever since we have been operating the service. The Persian Government insist upon Persian operators being employed, and we have the greatest difficult in ensuring that watch is kept even at the times when an aircraft is flying on the sector of which Jask is the centre. On two occasions the wireless station has been completely put out of action by careless use, or perhaps misuse, of the apparatu

As to the ability of the aircraft to maintain height on two out of three engines, it has been demonstrated time after time that i is quite possible. I cannot at the moment offer an explanation of why in the particular case in question it did not do so, but I imagin that the factor, that was influencing the one engine which stopped, wa also present, but not quite to such a serious degree, in the other en gines, and I take it they were not giving their full power.

The condition of affairs at Jask seems very unsatisfactory and I do not understand why there should have been no ice at Jask. We have already provided both an electric refrigerator and an "Icybal refrigerator for Jask, in order that ice shall be available.

At the moment conditions in Persia are almost unbelievably

Keith A. Pearson, Esq.,

difficult. As perhaps you know, the Persian Government have just introduced a series of new laws covering the operation of limited liability companies and very stringent import and export laws. For a time we could not even import food for our passengers who stayed the night at Jask without exporting a similar value of Persian produce. The actual value need not have imposed any serious obstacle, but the procedure for importation, in effect, amounted to a prohibition. Fortunately, we now have a special dispensation allowing us to import food for our passengers, but it is definitely refused for our own staff who live at Jask.

I imagine, therefore, that the importation of a spare part, for example for the refrigerator or for the self starter of the car, is, in effect, prohibited.

You may perhaps know that our authority to fly across Persia at all expires in March next. Negotiations are at present being carried on, in spite of very considerable discouragement, for the extension of the permission or for the continuance of the India service by another route.

Your criticism regarding lunch boxes at Karachi appears to admit of no possible valid explanation or excuse, and I am taking this up very strongly and immediately. I am also sorry to hear that our representation in India in general appears to be weak: I will see what can be done to overcome this difficulty.

I should like finally to offer you the Company's apologies for the inconvenience to which you were put owing to your landing at Jask, and once again to express our very cordial thanks to you for your very helpful letter.

Yours faithfully,

H Burchall

Assistant General Manager.

Keith A. Pearson, Esq.,
32 Victoria Street,
Westminster, S.W.1.

WHAT IS A PRESERVED RAILWAY ?

The granting of planning permission to operate trains across the level crossing at Sheringham, thus linking the North Norfolk to the commercial network raises some questions, in particular how we define different types of railway.

The origin of the term 'preserved' probably lies with the Talyllyn Railway Preservation Society which kept an existing railway running. However in most cases the railway has already closed and may even have been removed, in which case it is more accurate to use the word 'restored'.

Since the Railways Act of 1993 it has become legally necessary to distinguish a preserved railway from a commercial line since all are now private.

At this time the term 'heritage' was being used increasingly, and the change of the ARPS to HRA gave expression to this. It has the merit of covering all of that group of railways, not only preserved or restored but in some way historic such as the Snowdon Mountain Railway.

In 2006 officialdom defined a heritage railway as one which is operated to;

a. preserve, re-create or simulate railways of the past; b. demonstrate or operate historical or special types of motive power or rolling stock , exclusively or primarily for tourist, educational or recreational purposes.

A heritage railway is therefore mainly defined by its purpose. Abroad the definition varies, but heritage railways are normally defined as museum or tourist railways. In some cases it is museums which operate the railway. In others it is the local authorities which operate them. In most countries they have more power than they have in Britain. In Denmark, Ireland and Japan support is provided by the local national railway. In Austria commercial companies often run historic trains (and trams). In Ireland most heritage trains operate on the public railway.

In Britain the picture is becoming less clear. The idea of the Community Railway where local authorities work with a heritage line are becoming apparent. Furthermore the beginning of the operation of trains over public and heritage lines as envisaged in Sheringham is changing the picture further. As this tendency spreads it will place pressure on the volunteer ethos of the traditional heritage line. Heritage Railways will have to become more professional. The pressures of the law, health and safety, and consumers will require a different class of management.

2008

POLITICS AND PRESERVATION

In Britain we have been disinclined to use the preservation of artefacts for any national or political purpose. We have named locomotives after heroes and occasionally buildings after victorious battles, but these have been celebrations rather than deliberate reminders. On the continent there has been a much greater tendency to use streets, buildings and airports to remember political events and people.

In France railway wagons have been used to recall the dreadful use of these vehicles for transporting Jewish people to extermination camps.

These wagons were originally used in World War I for the carriage of troops to the front line. They bore a notice inside limiting capacity to 8 horses lengthways or 40 men.

Their use for transporting Jewish people has prompted a response which has sought to have examples preserved as a reminder, not only of the horrors but also of duplicity, of the split motivation of SNCF management under political instruction, of heroic disobedience by staff and crews, and the sickening attitude of the Nazi command, punishing subordinates for failing to provide a complete trainload of victims at the prescribed time.

Preserved wagon used for transporting Jewish people.

'THAT OLD SINNER'

With no relation to the previous article, this refers to the title of a book describing the history of the Letterkenny & Burtonport Extension Railway, which ran across northern Donegal from 1903 to 1947. This little known railway had a turbulent history and the book deserves to be read for many reasons: the operation of trains in wild country, with gale force winds blowing trains off the track, tales of violence and prejudice, of government attempts to relieve poverty, of relations between investors and a government department controlled by the Treasury. It gives a picture on the ground of life in the 'troubles' under a chairman obsessive about cost control and the dividend, for which services he was made a baronet.

The station at Gweedore in the far north west of Ireland on the Letterkenny & Burtonport Extension Railway. It shows the irregularity of the track and a sense of the remoteness, and in the distance the ominous shape of the mountain Erigal.

SHETLAND EXTREMES

This is a land of open moorland, gentle rolling hills, and long inlets from the sea, which is never more than three miles away. It has only 22,000 inhabitants. It was a surprise to see on a distant hillside in the far north what looked like an airplane. Investigation revealed the fuselage of a small airliner in a farmyard. In 1981 a French Potez 840 with five passengers and a crew was on its way from Edinburgh to Stornoway. Unfortunately Stornoway was closed on Sundays so the airplane was diverted to Sumburgh on Shetland. The landing-gear jammed during the landing and the propellers were damaged. It could not fly.
24 years later it had lost much of its equipment and had filled with blown sand and bird muck. It had been designed as a DC 3 replacement and only one other survived, in a museum near Paris. In 2002 the runway was to be extended so the Potez was required to be moved which meant scrapping it. A farmer living in the far north of the Main Island hired a large lorry and transported the airplane to his farm. There he is restoring it to a presentable state.

2007

The Potez 840, a 1946 Standard 12 in a woollen mill and Unst Boat Museum .

CONCORDE

The decision to withdraw Concorde from service raises some tricky questions for preservationists. It had become something of a legend in its lifetime, rather like a Routemaster bus. Sir Richard Branson spoke publicly about how its best future would be to preserve one of the 18 survivors as a flier, using the remaining carcasses as a source of spare parts. However BA, the owner, decided to preserve the British examples as non-fliers. The cost will be high as they insist that since they are in BA colours they must be well maintained. The TT has always had a preference for allowing preserved transport to be operated, so the Virgin solution had some appeal. Safe operation is more easily achieved in the case of a bus or a train, but there will always be examples where ultimately the fabric is too valuable to risk in operation. In the case of Concorde the burden of cost would have been very high.

However the alternative is not without problems. With at least nine Concordes in museums attracting funds, these funds will no longer be available for other aircraft preservation. Of course one must be preserved, or even two, but how many more ? The problem of supporting the cost of multiple examples applies as well to buses and railway engines. This is not a problem as long as there are individuals able to bear the cost. But when items of transport become dependent on grants, the only justification for multiple examples has to be operational, for the travel experience. Sometimes this is best provided by a replica such as London's horse bus, Shuttleworth's box-wing biplane, or the A1 locomotive 'Tornado' now under construction.

The demise of Concorde brings into the limelight yet another dilemma for preservationists. At a recent auction £320,000 was happily paid for a Concorde nose-cone, and £1200 for a Concorde blanket. Such sums would be valuable contributions to the cost of, say, a hangar. But it is a fact that it is human passions which have funded much transport preservation, and those emotions have little to do with logic. Only a few people will grab a cheque book because of the need for covered storage or a new roof. Yet without these many more items are at risk. Those of us who seek to bring order and reason into the preservation process do so against the grain of human character.

2003

LONDON'S FIRST TERMINUS

The London & Greenwich Railway, the first into London, was opened between Spa Road and Deptford on the 8 February 1836. It was delayed in reaching London Bridge by work on a bridge over Bermondsey Street caused by the late arrival of iron work from Dudley. London Bridge was reached on the 14 December 1836 and Greenwich in 1838.

The whole railway was built on brick arches, initially with two tracks. During its brief spell as a terminus the trains at Spa Road were reached by what was described as a flimsy stairway up the south side of the brick arcade; there was no platform and the booking office was at ground level.

Spa Road closed in December 1838 but in 1840 it was decided to re-open it. As the viaduct was being widened on the south side, the stairway had to be moved to the north side. In 1845, following the lease of the railway to the South Eastern, further alterations were made. A single platform was made with access from within the arch. The doorway although bricked up is still identifiable.
The station closed in 1872 and was replaced by another further down the line called Spa Road & Bermondsey. This had two platforms and access up stairs within the arch. 2011

MAUD

I have forgotten why we called her Maud when I bought her in 1953. She was a 1929 Morris Cowley, and had been used by the village hardware store for delivering paraffin, creosote and other noxious liquids available at that time in metal cans. On the death of Mr Barnard the owner, his daughter, who like most women of the time was unable to drive, put the car up for sale. I was still at school and Richard Wood, a friend who lived in the same village and who later designed jet engines for Rolls Royce, joined me in buying the car. His account of her restoration captures the atmosphere of the 50s, of a world where repair came before replace, where car ownership was rare, and when life moved at a gentler pace. Over to Richard:

' During the 1953 Summer term Denis Dunstone wrote to me at boarding school to tell me that old Barnard's Morris was up for sale and Bertram Guest, the local garage owner, was selling it for £7-10-0. I had had a birthday recently and sent off a postal order for £3-15-0. Home for half term I told my father of the purchase and he was furious. Fortunately Mr Dunstone senior bought my share. Later I was able to buy on my own account a Bentley for £130.

Maud, so named after the wife of Lord Nuffield, was a flat- nosed Cowley with a 2-seater fixed head coupe body with a dicky, registration number MM 9355. She was in bad condition and not running when we took her over. But her chrome radiator shell was magnificent and she came

with the original instruction book. Maud was moved and we decided the first thing to do was to carry out a decoke and valve grind. Easy job being a side-valve engine. Head off, valve chest cover off, and then I noticed that the magneto drive skew gear was worn to a knife edge. I took the magneto back to school to clean it up and to make HT leads- bright red. I had found in the school library a pre-war motoring book with a longitudinal section of a Cowley engine and gearbox. This I studied intently (no photocopiers then) but not intently enough, as will be recounted later.
We borrowed a valve compressor from the ever helpful Mr Guest and attempted to compress the springs to remove the collets. We nearly broke the clamp.
Once that was sorted it was plain sailing. Everything was ground in and cleaned up and reassembled. Time for a test. I dont think Denis was present and a friend came over in his mother's Austin A40 and towed us round the village. We had no exhaust manifold fitted so were expecting a big noise, but all we got was a few pops and bangs.

In doing this work I had noticed that the crankshaft had at least a 1/8th inch end float, if not more. So the decision was taken to look for another engine. We took the old engine out using a tripod and chain hoist. Having unbolted everything we could not get the engine to come away from the clutch. Even Mr Guest was mystified. Eventually we had to disconnect all the clutch springs through the inspection aperture in the bell-housing. This was a detail I had missed on the section drawing in the school library.

Before Denis went into the Navy for two years we found and bought a new engine for £2-10-0 in a Croydon scrapyard. Then nothing much was done until early 1955 when we found the roof had collapsed and the market gardener wanted the space. Fortunately a friend lived at a nearby house with a coach house, too small for the family car but big enough for Maud.

Now the real work started. We stripped the engine down and found it was in pretty good condition except that one piston was smashed at the rings. We took all the pistons to a supplier in Croydon who could provide new rings but not a new piston. However he suggested we took it to an aluminium dealer in South Croydon who could build it up and they would then machine it. While I was on holiday my friend put the engine back in the car. I then found a better float-chamber for the SU carburettor in a Reigate scrap-yard and persuaded a school friend to come and stay and rewire the car.

Meanwhile we started on the roof. An old gate post came in for the main cross member and after some splendid carpentry we finished with a new roof covered in rexine.
An illegal trip on the highway showed that the brakes needed attention. For £20 they were relined and also gaitered on the outside.
On returning from the Navy in 1956, Denis taxed and insured the car before going up to Cambridge, and we had several runs in her. She was easy to drive. A quiet start with the dynastart and the 3 speed crash gear-box was a delight. Even the pneumatic light dipper worked.'
I used Maud as my transport when I started work in London in 1959, and drove her every day from South Kensington to the City where I could park her outside the office. When I moved to Bristol I sold her for £15.

APPLIED PRESERVATION IN SUSSEX

At the closed Petworth Station in Sussex there is an admirable preservation scene. The station has been converted into a comfortable and interesting small hotel. Preserved with the building are a number of items and photographs from the time it was in use as a railway station. It was in fact the second station here having replaced the original which was a terminus in 1890.

There are three Pullman carriages available as double bedrooms.

THE 20 YEAR RULE ?

A discovery among the files in the National Archive at Kew set me thinking about the role of chance in preservation. An 1866 Working Timetable of the Sirhowy Railway, a coal carrier in South Wales, had been sent in 1888 by the station master at Tredegar to his boss at Abergavenny with a penned note across the top, 'Curiosity, 22 years old.' No doubt it had been lying at the bottom of a drawer until a new occupant of the desk was clearing his predecessors' accumulated paper clips, rubbers and pencil stubs. What twist of fate had caused this, at the time, unremarkable document to end up with Magna Carta among the records of the nation ? After 22 years a servant of the London & North Western Railway (which had taken over the Sirhowy) felt it had acquired a curiosity value. And because it had been lying in that desk for over 20 years, he filed it.

I was reminded of an action I had taken previously when getting my 1962 Rover 100 back on the road after 20 years in store. In the glove box I had come across the 1975 tax disc. Unconsciously I put it back. There it remained. Somehow it was too old to throw away.

If this rule applies to ephemera, perhaps it also has relevance for larger items. Most preserved items are preserved when at least 20 years old. Only the museums appear to have the objectivity to preserve anything new like a prototype HST. In the Essex village where I live it was decided that for the forthcoming Millennium a collection of everyday articles would be placed in the County Record Office in the expectation that in say 100 years time a researcher would find it as valuable as treasure trove.

1998

25 GWR COLLIES

Document RAIL 1005 385 in the National Archives contains an exchange of correspondence, which has survived, perhaps surprisingly, but which reveals an admirable display of courtesy by the Secretary of the GWR towards one of its more eccentric shareholders. Early in 1937 The Times had reported that the GWR had bought 25 collies to assist in keeping sheep off the track in the Welsh valleys. Mrs Sophia Heard was a shareholder who lived at Hassocks in Sussex and bred collies. She wrote to the GWR in a large and colourful hand on her AGM Proxy Form to complain at the GWR's cruelty to animals. She was haunted by the idea of the dogs being killed by the trains and almost wept at the thought of 'their courage and cleverness, waiting on the line until the men were in safety, and warning them of approaching trains'. She loved collies 'beyond everything'. Her own dogs were thoroughbreds, 'exquisite in every way and gold with white necks and chests.......devoted to me alone.'

Mr F.R.E.Davies replied on behalf of the company in calm and measured tones, noting the change of the shareholder's address, and enclosing an article from the GWR magazine which explained more fully how the dogs were to be employed.

This prompted an effusive reply from Mrs Heard. In a humble volte face she expressed amazement that Mr Davies had had time to reply to what she termed her 'untidy communication', and went on to say how much more comfortable she now felt.

She had imagined 'those darling dogs being caught between these sort of monsters doing 60, 70, and 80 m.p.h.' She went on to offer to the dogs food and balnkets, including 'good English buttock (raw) and eggs'. She enclosed a postal order payable to the the GWR for 1s 6p for the purchase of some Spratts dog biscuits, and requested a colour print of a GWR locomotive- 'not the ugly streamlined'. She already had pictures of 'Flying Scotsman' and 'Royal Scot', but nothing from 'the leading line of the world'. She expressed regret at having recently moved away from GWR territory and having to be content with 'hateful (twice underlined) electric trains.'

Mr Davies' reply was brief but courteous and enclosed a colour print as requested. This elicited a further outpouring of enthusiasm for the GWR, at the expense of the Southern. This moved Mr Davies to make a further reply, offering to make arrangements for Mrs Heard to see the GWR dogs, should she make the journey to Wales.

Mr Davies may have regretted this move as, far from putting a polite end to the exchange, Mrs Heard replied saying she had posted some Spratts dog biscuits to GWR headquarters, though her own dogs preferred 'very thin slices of brown bread, baked in the oven.'

Ever a gentleman, Mr Davies thanked her for the biscuits which had come to hand in excellent condition and had been forwarded to the Rhymney.

If Mr Davies had expected that to be the end of the matter, he was wrong. Mrs Heard was impressed by Mr Davies' kindness and orderly mind, 'which was so well balanced, otherwise you would not be in the position you are. I wonder if you would like some of my apples, or have you a country garden of your own ? Let me know on a postcard if you would.'

At this Mr Davies took a firm line. 'Thank you for your appreciative letter of yesterday and for your kind enquiry with reference to apples. I am however rather unfortunately placed in this respect and, much as I appreciate your gesture, I will ask you in the circumstances to excuse me from availing myself of it.'

The file does not record the nature of Mr Davies's 'circumstances', whether a large fruit farm or a delicate stomach, as at this point the correspondence appears to have ceased.

It was not quite the end of the story as by November 1938 Bob Martins, a rival of Spratts, were using the collies on the railway as the story-line for a newspaper advertising campaign.

1998

VOLVO 80th

The first production Volvo was manufactured in 1927 as a result of cooperation between Gustaf Larsen, a clever engineer and Assar Gabrielsson a wealthy business man. He purchased from his former employer, SKF, a dormant company called AB Volvo together with an abandoned factory near Gothenburg. The first car, an open four seater, bore a distinctive symbol on its radiator derived from the chemical symbol for iron, and the planet Mars. This symbol of the ring and arrowhead had to be suspended somehow and hence came the diagonal bar, which later became the most recognised feature of the logo. The saloon version was the first car to enable the back of the front seats to lie flat- for sleeping.   2007

The first Volvo, note left hand drive.

WELSH PHOENIX

The Corris was the first narrow gauge railway in Wales. It opened in 1859 carrying slate down to the River Dyfi. From 1883 to 1948 it also carried passengers to its own station at Machynlleth. Its two steam engines were sold to the Talyllyn, as no one expected them ever to be needed on the Corris. However in 1967 some Talyllyn supporters started investigating the possibility of creating a museum to record the story of the Corris.
In 1985 a train was operated over less than a mile of restored track. In 2003 the first public train was run, hauled by one of the locomotives sold to the Talyllyn. In 2005 a replica locomotive No. 7 was completed. This remarkable gradual process has been masterminded by the quietly determined David Coleman.   2010

No 7 and David Coleman

Corris Railway No. 3 sold in 1950 to the Talyllyn for £25. Few would have expected it to be back on the Corris again 60 years later

LANCASTER STATION

The railway reached Lancaster from Preston, 20 miles south, in 1840. The station in Lancaster was a fine handsome stone building which looked as though it was built to remain as a terminus for ever. Yet it was already clear that the country was about to be served by a network of lines between England and Scotland. Within four years the railway on to Carlisle was authorised. When the first station was by-passed it became a goods station and later a nurses' home in connection with the nearby hospital. It is still standing and in use, a good example of preservation in alternative use. But why was it built as a terminus ?

The explanation may lie in York. At the time that Lancaster was being linked to the railway system, a similar terminal station was being built at York. It seems that in the early days gaining access to the centre of a town was more important than having a through station. For one thing the range of locomotives was limited and frequent changes of locomotive were necessary. Secondly towns were reluctant to have a railway passing through the centre and it was easier to approach close to the centre with a terminus. Cambridge, Winchester and Exeter are examples of an early through station being located out of town. Urban sprawl has later embedded them in the town.

Very few termini survive in large towns, other than Glasgow, Liverpool and Manchester. Most survivors are near the coast. At York the original terminus is now offices.

London opposed through stations and it took 40 years from nationalisation before a through main line railway was available. Crossrail is more underground than surface railway.

The first station in Lancaster, now a nurses' home.

Part of the original plan of Lancaster Station.

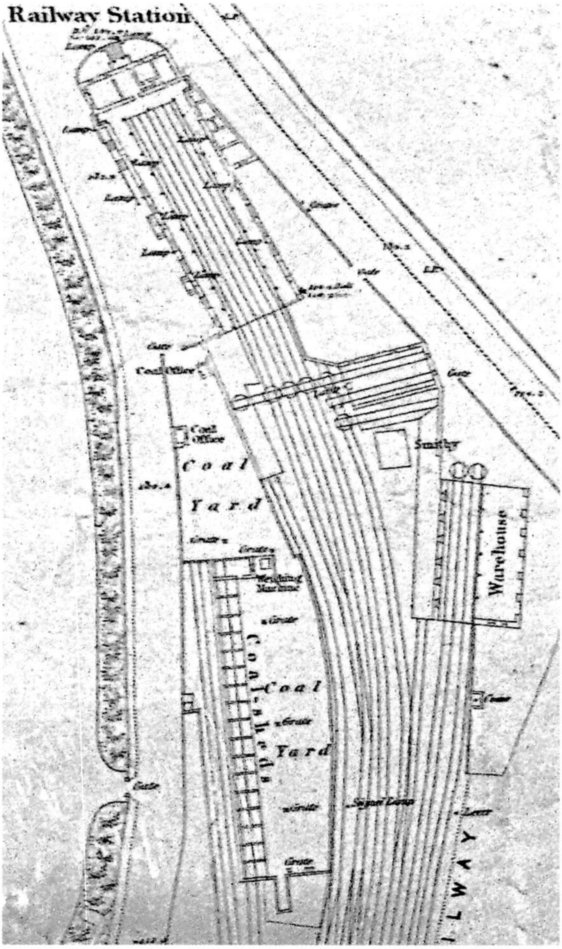

The original station at Lancaster. Note the size of the coal yard, and a large ware house, a smithy and what looks like a wagon turntable.

BISHOPSGATE GOODS STATION

The Victorian Society arranges visits to the wide variety of Victorian buildings still standing at locations all over the country. One of the more unusual of these occured recently when some 50 people gathered under the dripping arches over Wheler Street in the East End of London to examine the remains of what was once a massive railway complex. Those who have travelled by train into Liverpool Street Station may have wondered why the modern railway burrows through old brick cuttings and dismal caverns on its way to the glittering palace that is the renovated modern station.

The purpose of this visit was to try to find the answer and to discover what remains of what was originally called Shoreditch Station, the London terminus of the Eastern Counties Railway when it opened in 1839. Very little of Shoreditch remains because the handsome passenger terminal (see right) at a height of 40 ft. above the ground and approached up impressive stairways from the street was closed in 1875 on the opening of Liverpool Street Station. It had been necessary to extend the line into the City as the railway was losing passengers, unwilling to risk the dangers of penetrating into the rough quarter east of the City.

Liverpool Street Station was built at a low level to allow direct access to the Metropolitan Railway. In 1846 Shoreditch, which had been inaccurately renamed Bishopsgate in an attempt to mislead the public into believing it was closer to the City than it really was, became redundant, and was pulled down. In its place was constructed a massive two storey goods station. Wagons were lowered on hoists from the upper rail level to ground level for unloading. Over the following years this activity was extended over 10 acres with a third of this space providing cover for 165 wagons.

Over 500 horses were accommodated and by 1900 1,000 tons of garden peas were being handled in one July day. This activity continued until 1964 when a fire occurred in a liquor store.

When the line to Liverpool Street was put in, four tracks burrowed under the goods station, and platforms for a Bishopsgate passenger station were built under it. These are still discernible. Two more tracks were later laid under the goods station.

Today nothing is left of the goods station and like so many other redundant railway sites, it is now a car park. But the iron gates remain with the Great Eastern coat of arms and the weighbridge house, and the approach roads still follow the curve of the approach to the original station. It is hoped that the space under the arches can be developed and used for the extension of the East London Railway, if and when it is built.

Some of the arches are the fourth oldest railway structure in Britain, but it has to be admitted that the main reason for the survival of this massive monument to Victorian engineering is the cost of removing it.

1998

PRESERVATION IN ROMANIA

Not far from the Ukrainian border in the north of Romania is the last of the European forest railways. It augments its income by running tourist trains for 30 km. up a picturesque valley leading into the Carpathians. It has three 0-8-0 locomotives and a 0-6-0 and its passenger stock is from the Wengen Bahn in Switzerland and still bears the destination boards. In fact the railway is supported by Swiss preservation enthusiasts.
2011

The end of the line

Fuelling

Renault rail car

20th CENTURY VIKING SHIP

A replica of a Viking ship of 1,000 years ago is to be sailed to Dublin from Roskilde in Denmark. The ship which is a reconstruction of one of five dug up in the Roskilde fjord in 1962, is expected to cast light on Viking seamanship. It is believed that the original ship was built in Dublin and it has been suggested that she sailed to bring relief from Denmark to the English at the time of the Norman Conquest. Her name is 'Havhingsten' which means 'Sea Stallion'. 2007

A COCKTAIL OF INTERNATIONAL PRESERVATION

Stretched 'Trabby' made out of two of them, on display in Dresden.

Young driver in Leipzig

Tashkent Museum in Uzbekistan

Elbe paddle steamer near Dresden

Austrian electrics

Driver's view Stalingrad

On a journey by train from Moscow to Peking via Stalingrad, now Volgagrad, a ride in the cab revealed the size and height of Russian rolling stock. At this point the line to the left heads for Vladivostok, to the right for Tashkent and China.

MOTORING HISTORY

Considering the level of interest in the motor car and its international success as a means of transport, it is remarkable that so little has been written about its social history. Lavish large scale photographic studies have been produced and histories of makers and makes, but they normally pay most attention to technical matters. Yet it is the social impact especially in the early days which is more generally interesting. Recently I was rather surprisingly reminded of the social history when motoring in the mountains of western Norway. One of the most popular tourist locations in the area is a little village called Geiranger. It lies at the end of its fjord, a branch off the larger Storfjord, which leads into the North Sea. Its only connection with the rest of the world was formerly by water, as it is surrounded by mountains rising steeply to over 1,000 meters. The first cruise ship arrived in this remote location in 1869 and the local inhabitants were quick to see the potential for taking tourists up into the mountains in horse-drawn carriages to enjoy the views. This involved the construction of a steep road with narrow hairpin bends into mountain terrain over 1,500 m high. This was completed in 1889 and gave Geiranger road access to the rest of Norway, but only in the summer.

In the 1920s the inhabitants of the village saw the potential of the motor car as an enhancement of the tourist experience. Attempts to build a car locally were unsuccessful so some of the more enterprising clubbed together to buy three American seven-seater tourers. This proved a success as these massive machines were powerful enough to climb the hills yet nimble enough to get round the bends. The business thrived and it was said that Geiranger had more cars per head than anywhere else in the world.
The owner of one of the hotels in the village has collected nine of these ancient American cars and has brought them back to Geiranger. Eight have been restored and they are on display in his hotel. The collection consists of a 1919 Cadillac, a rare 1918 Mercer, a 1922 unrestored Hudson, two Studebakers from 1925 and 1932, a 1931 Nash, , three Buicks, from 1927, 1931, and 1932, and an A-Ford truck from 1932. They are run in the summer in local rallies.
2012

A 1931 Buick standing in the foyer of the Union Hotel in Geiranger.

ROAD SIGNS

This was a topic which never took off. I tried to set it going with the two signs opposite. Maybe the Editor did not find it as interesting as I did. With contributions from readers it might have become quite entertaining.

A rare example

Survivor near home

A once common sight

AA sign

Cayman Islands

Iceland

An illegal sign welcoming the traveller to the Serbian republic within Bosnia.

A once common AA village sign

Romanian fortified church in Transylvania

Welcome back.

A long way from anywhere in Kazakhstan

Steep hill in Harlech, Wales

Dogs, please note.

Street sign in St Croix, until 1917 a Danish colony, and retaining the Danish street name.

APPLIED PRESERVATION

In other words finding a use for an item which will fund its preservation. The three examples here of double deck buses across the world demonstrate variety. Photographed in 2005 in the American Virgin Islands, in 2006 in Cayman and in 2008 in Leipzig; the latter looks the most secure.

St Croix, US Virgin Isles

Cayman Islands

Leipzig

ELECTRIC TRAIN PRESERVATION

In 2008 the TT was stirred to take an initiative in preserving the electric train by the sight of Southern electric stock standing 1300 ft. up in the mountains of South Wales. Two Brighton Belle cars in Scotland on the Keith & Dufftown Railway emphasised the problem, which was, essentially, how can an electric train be preserved in running order?...and run.

The Nene Valley Railway had a collection of foreign locomotives which needed carriages with air brakes. Southern electric stock was so fitted and accordingly a train was made up of Southern electric carriages which included a Brighton Belle car.

This was better than standing in the garden of a Derbyshire pub.

In 1977 an attempt was made to create a museum for the Brighton Belle in the Pullman workshops in Brighton. A group of Belle cars was assembled for the purpose.

The prospect of saving in a museum looked good.

Unfortunately the project was badly vandalised and was given up. The cars awaited another saviour. This turned out to be James Sherwood of Sea Containers who incorporated three trailers in the VSOE steam train.

Being towed on a Heritage Railway seemed the only other solution, here on the North Norfolk in 1997.

The Brighton Belle train presented the best chance of a working vintage electric. It had in its favour all-steel carriages, a degree of fame and affection, and miraculously 14 of the original 15 cars still surviving. It would need new running gear, new motors, new coupling, new lavatories, much repair to interiors and, if it was to run on electric track, it would need compliance with a whole new world of signalling and safety devices.............and alot of cash.

In the future this scene at Streatham Hill by Mike Turner could theoretically be replicated, as a 4SUB exists, though in poor shape, and a 2BIL is in the National Railway Museum